The month of April, from the illuminated manuscript *Les Trés Riches Heures du duc de Berry*

The Story of a Special Day
Volume 92

April

1

91st day of the year
(92nd in leap years)
274 days remaining
until the end of the year.

by Michael Dobson

Timespinner
Press

Table of Contents

Cover: A French postcard for April Fools' Day. In France and other countries, the phrase "April fish!" is used in place of "April Fools!"

Otto von Bismarck, painting by Franz von Lenbach, 1894

April 1 Quotations

"The first of April is the day we remember what we are the other 364 days of the year."

— *Mark Twain (Samuel Langhorne Clemens)*

"When you want to fool the world, tell the truth."

— *Otto von Bismarck, born April 1, 1815*

"To joke in the face of danger is the supreme politeness, a delicate refusal to cast oneself as a tragic hero."

— *Edmond Rostand, born April 1, 1868*

"I suppose it is tempting, if the only tool you have is a hammer, to treat everything as if it were a nail."

— *Abraham Maslow, born April 1, 1908*

"It is no use to blame the looking glass if your face is awry."

— *Николáй Гóголь (Nikolai Gogol), born April 1, 1809*

"If you're going to do something stupid—and we all do—it might as well be a brave and foolish thing."

— *Samuel R. Delany, born April 1, 1942*

"Families are the best place to learn and practice mutual tolerance and acceptance."

— *Princess Inaara Aga Khan, born April 1, 1963*

An April Fools' Day prank: A fake subway car appears to break through the pavement in Copenhagen, Denmark, April 1, 2001. (Photo: Lars Andersen)

Event of the Day
April Fools' Day

April 1 is celebrated worldwide as April Fools' Day, when people play practical jokes and spread hoaxes. It's not uncommon for newspapers and other media to report fake stories. A good April Fools' Day prank should be good-humored and harmless, and when the prank is revealed, it's tradition to shout "April fool!"

There are a number of legendary April Fools pranks and hoaxes. The earliest known example of such a hoax dates back to 1698, when a number of people received tickets to the annual "Washing of the Lions" ceremony at the Tower of London—an event, of course, that does not exist—although tickets for it have been issued more than once.

In 1957, the BBC news show *Panorama* announced that the elimination of the "spaghetti weevil" meant that the Swiss were enjoying an unusually good spaghetti harvest—and showed footage of Swiss peasants appearing to pull strands of spaghetti from trees. In 1980, the same network reported that Big Ben, the famous clock tower in London, was going digital, and that the clock hands would be given away to the first four callers.

Of course, the BBC is far from the only news outlet to enjoy April Fools. In 2000, one newspaper reported the development of Viagra® for hamsters.

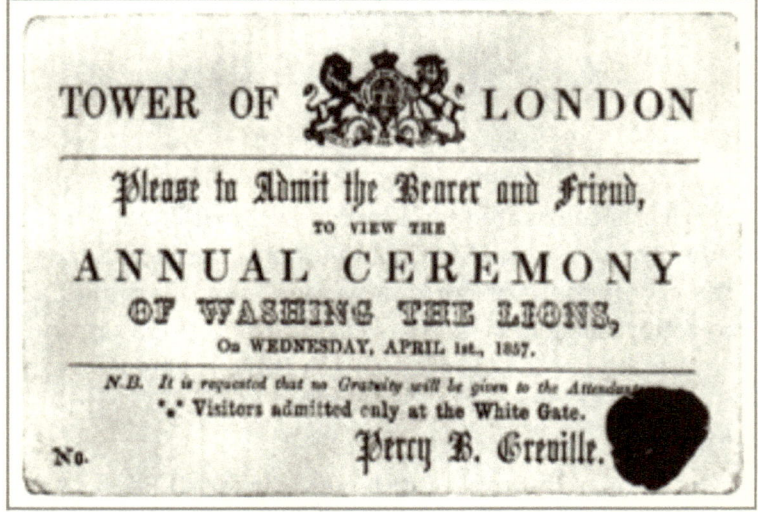

Admission ticket to the "Washing the Lions" ceremony, 1857

In 1987, a radio disc jockey in Los Angeles announced that all freeways would be closed for repairs, resulting in widespread panic. In 1998, the Guinness brewery announced they were now the official beer sponsors of the Greenwich Observatory, and that henceforth "Greenwich Mean Time" would be known as "Guinness Mean Time." Several newspapers printed the story, unaware it was a hoax.

Although April Fools' Day in its modern form first became popular in the 19th century (although it's not an official public holiday in any country), the earliest citation for April 1 as Fools' Day comes from Geoffrey Chaucer's *The Canterbury Tales*, first published in 1392, but the idea of a day for practical jokes and hoaxes goes back much further.

The Roman festival of Hilaria, celebrated on March 25 in honor of the goddess Cybele, gives rise to our word "hilarious." Hilaria comes from the Greek festival ΑΝΑΒΑΣΙΣ ("Ascensus"), a day of rejoicing, but oddly in the evening of that day it turns to ΚΑΤΑΒΑΣΙΣ ("Descensus"), a time spent in tears and lamentations.

Hilaria itself wasn't particularly hilarious, though it was definitely happy. Another precursor to April Fool's Day was the medieval Feast of Fools, in which a mock pope known as the Lord of Misrule was consecrated in a ceremony mocking the church. The Feast of Fools was variously held on December 13, December 28, and January 1, and its general celebration echoed the Roman Saturnalia.

The Feast of the Ass was celebrated in France on January 14, celebrating the donkey-related stories in the Bible, particularly the donkey that carried Jesus and family into Egypt. A donkey was usually brought into church and the congregation would say "Hee-Haw" instead of their normal responses during the service.

The Catholic Church banned the Feast of Fools in the Council of Basel in 1431. Early Protestants also condemned the festival, but there are documented instances of the feast held as late as 1644. The exact origin of April Fools' Day, however, remains in doubt. It's often suggested that the designation of January 1 as New Year's Day in the Gregorian calendar was responsible.

In Scotland, April 1 was once known as "Hunt-the-Gowk Day." (A "gowk" is a cuckoo or a foolish person.) A traditional prank was to ask someone to deliver a sealed message that supposedly requested help of some sort. However, the message actually read, "Dinna laugh, dinna smile Hunt the gowk another mile."

In Italy, France, and Belgium, people tack paper fishes on each other's backs and shout "April Fish!" A related Flemish custom is for children to lock out parents or teachers, letting them in for a promise of treats. In Poland, the tradition was so strong that an important treaty, actually signed on April 1, was backdated to March 31 so people wouldn't think it was a hoax.

Many countries celebrate a day of pranks and practical jokes, but not all of them take place on April 1.

In Spanish-speaking countries, December 28 is still celebrated as a day of pranks. The Danes and Swedes celebrate May 1 as well as April 1. Koreans were allowed to lie and fool each other on the first snowy day of the year.

Of course, not everybody thinks practical jokes are funny, and a number of critics have complained about the hobby. That's why it's important to make sure your own April Fools' Day pranks, if you decide to play along, are harmless and good-humored.

By the way, if you read this article backwards, it will give you a secret message!

April fool!

April 1 Holidays and Celebrations

Wan Kha Ratchakan Phonlaruean (Thailand)

Civil Service Day in Thailand commemorates the enactment of the first Civil Service Act in 1928.

Fossil Fools Day (International)

Fossil Fools Day (a play on "Fossil Fuels") is an environmental demonstration day. Various environmental groups sponsor events and displays promoting alternate energy and opposing the use of fossil fuels.

Kha b-Nisan (Assyrian people)

The Assyrian people, in Syria and elsewhere, celebrate the beginning of their new year on April 1.

National Sourdough Bread Day (United States)

In the United States, almost every day of the year is dedicated to a particular food. Sponsored by manufacturers, retailers, farmers, or simply fans, these days are often proclaimed by the President, Congress, state governors, or mayors.

April 1 is National Sourdough Bread Day. Although sourdough bread is most often associated with San Francisco, sourdough bread has been discovered in ancient sites dating back to 3700 BCE. Throughout human history, sourdough, a *lactobacillus* culture, was used instead of cultivated forms of yeast. Because flour contains a variety of natural yeasts and bacteria, if mixed with water and given time, it will form a dough with a characteristically sour taste. In addition to the San Francisco variety, rye bread, Amish friendship bread, pumpernickel, and Ethiopian *injera* all use a sourdough process.

Edible Book Day (International)

The International Edible Book Festival officially commemorates the birthday of French gastronome Jean Anthelme Brillat-Savarin, but it's also connected to April Fools' Day, because it's a great day to "eat your words." Participants create "edible books," which must integrate text or otherwise relate to actual books, which are eaten at the end of the festival. Festivals are held in a number of different cities around the globe.

Odisha Day (Utkala Dibasa) (Odisha State, India)

The Indian state of Odisha was eliminated as a separate political entity in 1568, but on April 1, 1936, the British established it as one of the 29 states that make up India. This is celebrated annually as Odisha Day (ଓଡ଼ିଶା ଦିବସ).

An edible book version of Ray
Bradbury's *Fahrenheit 451*.

Ruz e Jomhuri ye Eslāmi (Islamic Republic Day) (Iran)

Iran uses three different calendars, two solar and one lunar. The Persian calendar is used as the national calendar, the Gregorian calendar for international events and Christian holidays, and the Lunar calendar for Islamic holidays. Islamic Republic Day (روز جمهوری اسلامی) is celebrated on April 1, or Farvadin 12 on the Persian calendar.

Veneralia (ancient Rome)

The Romans honored Venus Verticordia ("Venus, the changer of hearts") and Fortuna Virilis ("Virile Fortune") on the Kalends of April (April 1). At the Veneralia, women and men asked Venus Verticordia for help in affairs of the heart.

Christian Feast Days

In *Western Christianity*, saints commemorated on April 1 include Cellach of Armagh, Hugh of Grenoble, Frederick Deinson Maurice (Episcopal Church), Melito of Sardis, Nuno Álvarez Pereira, Tewdrig, Theodora, and Abbot Walrich of Leuconay.

In *Eastern Orthodox Christianity*, it is the commemoration of Hermes and Theodora the martyrs, Melito of Sardis, Saint Mary of Egypt, Saint Procopius of Sázava, Tewdric of Tintern, Abraham of Bulgaria, Barsanuphius of Optina, and Joachim of Kyiv. (These are celebrated on April 14 by "Old Calendarists.")

Other Holidays

Some holidays are simply made up by individuals, companies, or other organizations, and whether they become widely adopted depends on whether people choose to celebrate them. Here are some opportunities to celebrate on April 1.

April 1 is:

- Boomer Bonus Day
- International Tatting Day
- Library Snap Shot Day
- Myles Day
- National Atheists Day
- National Fun Day
- National Soylent Green Day
- Poetry and the Creative Mind Day
- Reading is Funny Day
- Sorry Charlie Day
- St. Stupid Day
- US Air Force Academy Day.

The iconic Cadet Chapel at the United States Air Force Academy, Colorado Springs, Colorado. The Academy was established on April 1, 1954, by President Dwight D. Eisenhower

What Happened on April 1?

1789 – First Session of the House of Representatives

The United States Constitution, scheduled to come into effect on March 4, 1789, provided for a "bicameral" legislature, consisting of both a House of Representatives and a Senate. Because of delays in election and travel, the new House of Representatives was only able to achieve a quorum for the first time on April 1, 1789. Frederick Muhlenberg, a Pennsylvania Lutheran minister, was elected as the first Speaker of the House.

1824 – Singapore Becomes a Crown Colony

In 1819, Sir Thomas Raffles negotiated a treaty with the Sultan of Johor on behalf of the British East India Company to develop the southern part of the island of Singapore as a British trading post. By 1824, the British were in possession of the entire island, and it was declared a British Crown Colony following a second treaty with the Sultan. Singapore subsequently became one of the world's major commercial hubs, gaining its full independence from the United Kingdom in 1963. The name "Singapore" comes from the Malay word *Singapura*, which translates as Lion City, although it is unlikely that lions ever lived on the island.

1873 – RMS *Atlantic* Sinks

On April 1, 1873, the White Star transatlantic ocean liner RMS *Atlantic* ran onto rocks and sank off the coast of Nova Scotia. Of the 952 aboard the ship, only 371 survived. This was the deadliest civilian maritime disaster in the North Atlantic until the sinking of SS *La Bourgogne* in 1898, and the greatest disaster for the White Star line until the loss of RMS *Titanic* in 1912.

RMS *Atlantic*

1918 — The Royal Air Force is Founded

The British Royal Air Force, the oldest independent air force in the world, was founded toward the end of World War I on April 1, 1918. It merged two existing units, the Royal Flying Corps and the Royal Naval Air Service.

1924 — Adolf Hitler is Sentenced

Following the failure of the "Beer Hall Putsch," an attempted coup by the Nazi Party to take power in Munich, Bavaria, Nazi leader Adolf Hitler was arrested, charged with treason, and convicted after a 24-day trial that gave Hitler a platform to advance his ideas to the German nation. He was sentenced to five years in prison on April 1, 1924, but only served nine months of his sentence prior to being released, during which he wrote his manifesto *Mein Kampf*.

1939 — The Spanish Civil War Ends

The Spanish Civil War was fought between the Republicans, loyal to the Spanish Republic, and the Nationalists, a rebel group led by Generalissimo Francisco Franco and supported by Nazi Germany and Fascist Italy. After a brutal and bitter war, the Nationalist forces achieved victory on April 1, 1939, issuing in a 39-year dictatorship.

1945 — The Battle of Okinawa Begins

On April 1, 1945, the United States launched an invasion of the island of Okinawa in the largest amphibious assault in the Pacific during World War II. The campaign was known as Operation Iceberg in the US, and it is also known as *tetsu no ame* ("rain of steel) in Japanese.

In the 82-day campaign that followed, the Japanese military lost over 77,000 soldiers, the Allies over 14,000, and civilian death estimates range from 42,000 to 150,000.

This was the bloodiest battle of the Pacific War, and ended with an Allied victory. The war against Japan ended less than two months after the end of the battle, after the atomic bombings of Hiroshima and Nagasaki and the Soviet invasion of Manchuria. The United States continued to occupy Okinawa until 1972.

American landing craft unload supplies on an Okinawa beach.

1948 — The Soviets Blockade Berlin

In the first major crisis of the Cold War, the Soviet Union blocked access to the city of Berlin by the Western Allies. Although Berlin was located in East Germany, the city itself was under joint occupation by both the Soviet Union and the Western Allies (the US, Great Britain, and France). In response to the blockade, the Western Allies launched the Berlin Airlift to carry supplies to the Allied areas of West

American aircraft unloading supplies at Tempelhof Airport, Berlin

Berlin. In one year, over 200,000 flights delivered 8,000 tons of vital necessities each day. In May 1949, the Soviets lifted the blockade.

1954 — The US Air Force Academy is Established

On April 1, 1954, US President Dwight D. Eisenhower established a military service academy for the recently created United States Air Force. Located in Colorado Springs, Colorado, the Air Force Academy graduated its first class in 1959. It is one of the largest tourist attractions in Colorado, receiving over 1 million visitors a year.

1960 — First Picture of Earth from Space

On April 1, 1960, the Television Infrared Observation Satellite (TIROS-1) became the first successful low-orbit weather satellite. It transmitted the first television image of planet Earth taken from orbit. Although the TIROS-1 mission ended in June, TIROS satellites continue to provide weather data.

The first televised image of Earth from space, taken by TIROS-1

1960 — First Dr. Martens Boots

The popular brand of Dr. Martens boots first went on sale on April 1, 1960. Known as Style 1460, they are still in production today.

1969 — Hawker Siddeley Harrier Introduced

The first successful V/STOL (Vertical/Short Takeoff and Landing) jet, the Harrier Jump Jet, was introduced on April 1, 1969. It remained in active service until 2006.

1970 — Surgeon General's Warning Required

On April 1, 1970, US President Richard Nixon signed the Public Health Cigarette Smoking Act, which required a Surgeon General's warning printed on each cigarette package and banned cigarette advertisements on American radio and television.

1976 — Apple Computer Founded

On April 1, 1976, Steve Jobs, Steve Wozniak, and Ronald Wayne founded Apple Computer, Inc., to sell the Apple I personal computer kit. (Ronald Wayne later sold his share of Apple for $8,000.) Today, Apple is the largest publicly traded corporation in the world, as well as the world's largest technology company, valued at over $700 billion.

1979 — Iran Becomes an Islamic Republic

Following a series of demonstrations and strikes, the Shah of Iran fled the country and Ayatollah Ruhollah Khomeni (روح الله خمینی) returned from exile to become Supreme Leader of the country. The new government was officially declared an Islamic Republic after winning 99% of the vote in a referendum.

1997 — Comet Hale-Bopp Reaches Perihelion

Comet Hale-Bopp, the most widely observed comet of the 20th century, reached perihelion, the point in its orbit when it became closest to the Sun, on April 1, 1997, approximately two years since its discovery by astronomers. The comet was visible to the naked eye for a record-setting 18 months. It reached a point closest to planet Earth on March 22, 1997.

Comet Hale-Bopp

1999 — Nunavut Established

The newest territory of Canada, Nunavut, was established on April 1, 1999. Nunavut is both the least populated and the largest in area of the provinces and territories in Canada.

2001 — Slobodan Milošević Arrested

Serbian president Slobodan Milošević (Слободан Милошевић) was arrested by Yugoslav authorities on April 1, 2001, following a 36-hour armed standoff. He was extradited to The Hague to stand trial for war crimes before the International Criminal Tribunal, but died before his trial concluded.

2001 — Same-Sex Marriage Becomes Legal in the Netherlands

On April 1, 2001, the Netherlands became the first country in the world to legalize same-sex marriage.

2004 — Google Announces Gmail

On April 1, 2004, Google announced the public launch of its free email service, Gmail. At a time when other free email services offered 20-25 megabytes of storage, Gmail offered an initial 1 gigabyte of free storage, unheard of at the time. Because the announcement came on April 1, many thought it was an April Fools' Day joke.

Debbie Reynolds

Who Was Born on April 1?

Acting

Jon Gosselin (April 1, 1977 –)

Jon Gosselin achieved notoriety for his role with ex-wife Kate Gosselin and their eight children on the reality TV series *Jon & Kate Plus 8*.

Ali McGraw (April 1, 1939 –)

Actress Ali McGraw won the Golden Globe Award for Best Actress for her role in the 1970 film *Love Story*. Other other films include *Goodbye, Columbus, The Getaway*, and the television miniseries *The Winds of War*.

Debbie Reynolds (April 1, 1932 –)

Actress, singer, and dancer Debbie Reynolds is known for her roles in such films as *Singin' in the Rain, Tammy and the Bachelor*, and *The Unsinkable Molly Brown*. She is the mother of actress and author Carrie Fisher.

Grace Lee Whitney (April 1, 1930 – May 1, 2015)

Actress Grace Lee Whitney is best known for her role as Janice Rand on the original *Star Trek* television series.

Jane Powell (April 1, 1929 –)

Actress, singer, and dancer Jane Powell appeared in many MGM musicals, including *Royal Wedding*, with Fred Astaire, and *Seven Brides for Seven Brothers,* with Howard Keel.

Toshirō Mifune (April 1, 1920 – December 24, 1997)

Japanese actor Toshirō Mifune (三船 敏郎) is best known for the 16 films he made with Akira Kurosawa, including *Rashomon, Seven Samurai*, and *Yojimbo*. He played Lord Toronaga in the US television miniseries *Shōgun*.

Wallace Beery (April 1, 1885 – April 15, 1949)

Actor Wallace Beery made over 250 films during his 36-year career, winning the Academy Award for Best Actor for his title role in *The Champ*. His other well-known roles include Long John Silver in *Treasure Island* (1934) and Pancho Villa in *Viva Villa!* At the height of his career, he was the highest paid actor in the world.

Toshirō Mifune — movie poster for the 1950 Japanese film *Shubun (Scandal)*, released by Shochiku Company.

Lon Chaney in *The Phantom of the Opera* (1925)

Lon Chaney (April 1, 1883 – August 26, 1930)

Lon Chaney is best known for his roles in such silent horror films as The Hunchback of Notre Dame (1923) and The Phantom of the Opera (1925). Known as "the Man of a Thousand Faces," he played a wide range of characters in over 90 films. His son Creighton, later billed as Lon Chaney, Jr., was also known for his film portrayal of monsters.

Business and Manufacturing

Alexander Yakovlev (April 1 [O.S. March 19], 1906 – August 22, 1989)

Soviet aeronautical engineer Alexander Yakovlev (Алекса́ндр Я́ковлев) founded the Yakovlev Design Bureau, which developed fighter aircraft and civilian airliners for the Soviet Union during World War II and afterward, including one of the first Soviet jet aircraft. He later served as Vice-Minister of Aviation for the Soviet Union under Joseph Stalin.

James Fisk, Jr. (April 1, 1835 – January 7, 1872)

"Diamond Jim" Fisk was considered to be one of the "robber barons" of the Gilded Age, as the late 19th century is known. His attempt with Jay Gould and "Boss" Tweed to corner the gold market resulted in the stock market "Black Friday" of 1869, which created a scandal for the administration of President Ulysses S. Grant. He was murdered when an extortion scheme involving his mistress backfired. His story was fictionalized in the 1937 film *The Toast of New York*.

Crime and Punishment

Terry Nichols (April 1, 1955 –)

Terry Nichols was convicted as an accomplice in the bombing of the Alfred P. Murrah Federal Building in Oklahoma City, Oklahoma, in 1995. He was convicted of 161 counts of first degree murder and was sentenced to 161 consecutive life terms without the possibility of parole.

Music

Susan Boyle (April 1, 1961 –)

Scottish singer Susan Boyle's performance of "I Dreamed a Dream" from *Les Misérables* on the TV show *Britain's Got Talent* resulted in international attention.

Gil Scott-Heron (April 1, 1949 – May 27, 2011)

Soul and jazz poet Gil Scott-Heron was both a spoken word performer and musician. His best-known composition is "The Revolution Will Not Be Televised."

Jimmy Cliff (April 1, 1948 –)

Jamaican ska and reggae musician Jimmy Cliff was inducted into the Rock and Roll Hall of Fame in 2010.

Arthur "Guitar Boogie" Smith (April 1, 1921 – April 3, 2014)

Country music songwriter and performer Arthur Smith produced the first nationally syndicated country music show on television. He got his nickname for his biggest commercial hit, "Guitar Boogie." His song "Feudin' Banjos" was re-recorded as "Dueling Banjos" and used as the theme song for the movie *Deliverance*.

Eddy Duchin (April 1, 1909 – February 9, 1951)

Popular pianist and bandleader during the 1930s and 1940s, Eddie Duchin served as a US Navy officer during World War II but was unable to reestablish his stardom after the war. He died of leukemia at the age of 41. He is the subject the 1956 film *The Eddy Duchin Story*. His cover of the Louis Armstrong song "Ol' Man Mose" was banned in Great Britain because the singer's pronunciation of "bucket" was misunderstood.

Sergei Rachmaninoff (April 1 [O.S. March 20], 1873 – March 28, 1943)

Russian composer, pianist, and conductor Sergei Rachmaninoff (Сергей Рахманинов) is considered one of the last great representatives of Romanticism in Russian classical music. His better known compositions include his First Piano Concerto and the Prelude in C-Sharp Minor.

Sergei Rachmaninoff

Politics, Law, and Military

Rachel Maddow (April 1, 1973 –)

Television host, political commentator, and author Rachel Maddow hosts the MSNBC program *The Rachel Maddow Show*.

Samuel Alito (April 1, 1950 –)

Samuel Alito was named an Associate Justice of the US Supreme Court in 2006. He is known as a member of the conservative wing of the court.

Vladimir Posner (April 1, 1934 –)

Journalist and commentator Vladimir Posner (Влади́мир По́знер) was known for representing and explaining the views of the Soviet Union on American television during the Cold War.

Whittaker Chambers (April 1, 1901 – July 9, 1961)

A member of the Communist Party USA and a Soviet spy, Chambers renounced communism and became an outspoken opponent of it. He is best known for his role in the perjury and espionage trial of Alger Hiss, in which he hid microfilm evidence in a hollowed-out pumpkin. After the Hiss trial, he worked in various conservative media as a writer. President Ronald Reagan awarded him the Presidential Freedom Medal posthumously in 1984.

Clementine Ogilvy Spencer-Churchill (April 1, 1885 – December 12, 1977)

Lady Spencer-Churchill was the wife of Winston Churchill, and a baroness in her own right.

Otto von Bismarck (April 1, 1815 – July 30, 1898)

One of the great diplomats in history, Otto von Bismarck unified the German states into an empire under the leadership of Prussia. Historian Eric Hobsbawm wrote that Bismarck "remained undisputed world champion at the game of multilateral diplomatic chess." He was the first chancellor of the German Empire, controlling domestic and foreign affairs until being removed from power in 1890 by Kaiser Wilhelm II.

Science, Academics and Medicine

A. Q. Khan (April 1, 1936 –)

Pakistani nuclear physicist Abdul Qadeer Khan (ذاكثر عبد القدير خان) was a key figure in Pakistan's development of nuclear weapons.

Joseph Murray (April 1, 1919 – November 26, 2012)

Plastic surgeon Joseph Murray performed the first successful human kidney transplant and shared the Nobel Prize in Physiology or Medicine for his work on organ transplantation.

Abraham Maslow (April 1, 1908 – June 8, 1970)

Psychologist Abraham Maslow is best known for creating Maslow's Hierarchy of Needs, a theory of understanding and fulfilling innate human needs.

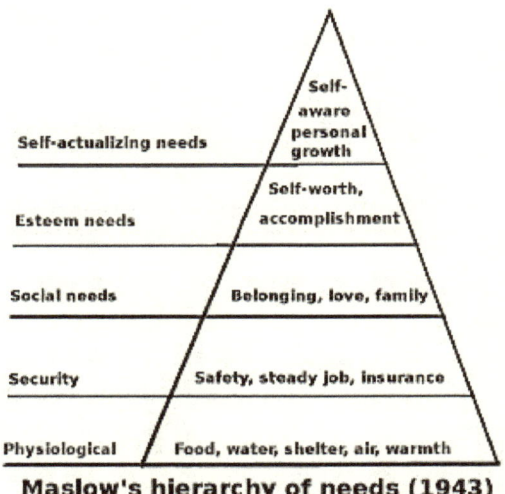

Maslow's hierarchy of needs (1943)

William James Sidis (April 1, 1898 – July 17, 1944)

Claimed to have the highest IQ ever recorded, child prodigy William James Sidis entered Harvard University at the age of eleven, and received his degree at the age of sixteen.

An outspoken pacifist, he was arrested for participating in a political rally and sentenced to 18 months in prison. Instead, his parents arrange for him to be committed to a sanitarium to "reform" him. He spent the remainder of his life working menial jobs and obsessively collecting streetcar transfers.

Sophie Germain (April 1, 1776 – June 27, 1831)

French mathematician, physicist, and philosopher Sophie Germain received the Grand Prize from the Paris Academy of Sciences for her mathematical work. Unable to make a career in mathematics because of prejudice against her sex, she continued to work independently. The Academy of Sciences later established the Prix Sophie Germain, given each year to a French mathematician for research.

William Harvey (April 1, 1578 – June 3, 1657)

English physician William Harvey was the first known person to describe in detail the circulation and other properties of blood.

Sports

Scott Stevens (April 1, 1964 –)

Hockey player Scott Sevens played 22 seasons in the National Hockey League, winning the Smythe Trophy as the MVP in the Stanley Cup playoffs in 2000. He was inducted into the Hockey Hall of Fame in 2007.

Bo Schembechler (April 1, 1929 – November 17, 2006)

Head football coach at Miami University (1963-1968) and the University of Michigan (1969-1989), Bo Schembechler achieved a career record of 234-65-8. He was inducted into the College Football Hall of Fame in 1993.

Words

Brad Meltzer (April 1, 1970 –)

Brad Meltzer is known for his best-selling political thrillers, beginning with 1997's *The Tenth Justice*.

Samuel R. Delany (April 1, 1942 –)

Author, professor, and critic Samuel R. Delany won four Nebula Awards and two Hugo Awards for such works as *Babel-17, The Einstein Intersection*, and *Dhalgren*. He was named a Grand Master by the Science Fiction Writers of America in 2013.

Milan Kundera (April 1, 1929 –)

Milan Kundera's best known work is *The Unbearable Lightness of Being*. His works were banned by the Communist government in Czechoslovakia, and Kundera has lived most of his life in exile in France.

Anne McCaffrey (April 1, 1926 – November 21, 2011)

Science fiction writer Anne McCaffrey is best known for her *Dragonriders of Pern* novels. She was the first woman to win a Hugo Award and the first to win a Nebula Award. She was named a Grand Master by the Science Fiction Writers of America.

William Manchester (April 1, 1922 – June 1, 2004)

Author and historian William Manchester's bestselling books include his account of the assassination of President John F. Kennedy, *The Death of a President*, and his biography of General Douglas MacArthur, *American Caesar*. He received the National Humanities Medal and the Abraham Lincoln Literary Award.

Edgar Wallace (April 1, 1875 – February 10, 1932)

English thriller writer Edgar Wallace is best remembered today for creating *King Kong*. In his prolific career, he authored more than 170 novels and sold over 50 million copies of his works worldwide.

Edmond Rostand (April 1, 1868 – December 2, 1918)

French poet and dramatist Edmond Rostand is best known for his play *Cyrano de Bergerac*. His play *Les Romanesques* was adapted into the musical comedy *The Fantasticks*.

John Wilmot (April 1, 1647 – July 26, 1680)

Poet, courtier, and satirist John Wilmot was considered one of the great wits of the Restoration, though much of his poetry was censored during the Victorian era. Known for his rakish lifestyle, he was the model for a number of such characters in literature, such as Don John in Shadwell's *The Libertine*.

Eleanor of Aquitaine (left), in the painting *Queen Eleanor and Fair Rosamond*, by Evelyn de Morgan. Eleanor of Aquitaine died on April 1, 1204

Who Died on April 1?

Art

Max Ernst (April 2, 1891 — April 1, 1976)

Painter and sculptor Max Ernst was one of the pioneers of the Dada movement and Surrealism, and influenced the development of abstract expressionism.

Business

Helena Rubinstein (December 25, 1872 — April 1, 1965)

Entrepreneur Helena Rubinstein founded the cosmetics company of the same name, becoming the first self-made female millionaire in the United States and one of the richest people in America. She was married to Edmund Titus, who published *Lady Chatterley's Lover,* and again to Prince Artchil Gourielli-Tchkonia.

Music

Cynthia Lennon (September 10, 1939 — April 1, 2015)

Cynthia Lennon was the first wife of Beatle John Lennon and the mother of musician Julian Lennon.

Marvin Gaye (April 2, 1939 — April 1, 1984)

Marvin Gaye's many Motown hits included "How Sweet It Is (To Be Loved By You)," "I Heard It Through the Grapevine," "What's Going On," and "Let's Get It On." He died after being shot by his father in 1984. He was honored posthumously with the Grammy Lifetime Achievement Award, and is a member of both the Rhythm and Blues Music Hall of Fame and the Rock and Roll Hall of Fame.

Marvin Gaye

Scott Joplin (c. 1867/68 — April 1, 1917)

African-American composer and pianist Scott Joplin, known as the "King of Ragtime Writers," wrote numerous songs, including one ballet and one opera. His best known work, "The Maple Leaf Rag," is featured, along with others of his songs, in the 1973 film *The Sting*. His ragtime opera, *Treemonisha*, was finally staged in 1972 to critical claim, and in 1976, Joplin was posthumously awarded a Pulitzer Prize.

Performing Arts

John Forsythe (January 29, 1918 – April 1, 2010)

John Forsythe is best known for his role as Blake Carrington on the prime time soap opera *Dynasty*, and as the voice of Charlie in the tv series *Charlie's Angels*.

Carrie Snodgress (October 27, 1945 – April 1, 2004)

Actress Carrie Snodgress received an Academy Award nomination and two Golden Globes for her 1970 appearance in *Diary of a Mad Housewife*. Other films include *Murphy's Law* and *Pale Rider*. She was married twice, once to musician Neil Young.

Martha Graham (May 11, 1894 – April 1, 1991)

Dancer and choreographer Martha Graham is one of the towering figures of modern dance. She has been called the "Picasso of Dance." She received numerous honors, including the Presidential Medal of Freedom and election as a Fellow of the American Academy of Arts and Sciences. *Time* Magazine named her "Dancer of the Century" in 1998.

Martha Graham, by Nickolas Muray

Jim Jordan (November 16, 1896– April 1, 1988)

Jim Jordan played Fibber McGee in the television series *Fibber McGee and Molly,* and was the voice of the albatross Orville in Disney's 1977 animated film, *The Rescuers.*

Jim Jordan (left) in *Fibber McGee and Molly*

Noah Beery, Sr. (January 17, 1882– April 1, 1946)

Actor Noah Beery, Sr., was the elder brother of actor Wallace Beery (see "Who Was Born on April 1") and the father of character actor Noah Beery, Jr..
Although less well known than his brother, he made around 70 films in his career.

Politics and Military

Eleanor of Aquitaine (1122 or 1124 — April 1, 1204)

One of the most powerful women in European history, Eleanor of Aquitaine was a duchess in her own right, highly educated, strong willed, and very wealthy. She was married first to King Louis VII of France, and after that marriage was annulled, married the man who became King Henry II of England. Her sons Richard I the Lionheart and John both later became Kings of England.

Her marriage to Henry II was turbulent, and for much of their time, they maintained separate courts. Eleanor's court became known as the "Court of Love," associated with the idea of courtly love.

After a revolt against Henry II by her son Henry the Young King, Eleanor was imprisoned by her husband for over sixteen years. It is claimed that Eleanor arranged for the death of Henry II's favorite mistress, Rosamund Clifford, known as "Fair Rosamund."

She lived through the entire reign of Richard I, acting as regent during his crusading, and well into the reign of her youngest son, King John.

Science and Medicine

Charles R. Drew (June 3, 1904 — April 1, 1950)

African-American physician Charles R. Drew was a leading authority in the field of blood transfusions.

He developed improved techniques for blood storage, and developed large-scale blood banks in World War II that saved thousands of lives. He protested against the practice of racial segregation in the donation of blood, as it had no scientific justification, resulting in him losing his job.

He died in a car accident. An often-repeated story that the Alabama hospital to which he was taken refused to give him a blood transfusion because of his skin color turns out to be false; his injuries were evidently so severe that no existing treatment could have saved him.

Hermann Rorschach (November 8, 1884 — April 1, 1922)

Swiss psychiatrist Hermann Rorschach is best known for creating the Rorschach inkblot test, designed to reflect unconscious part of the personality.

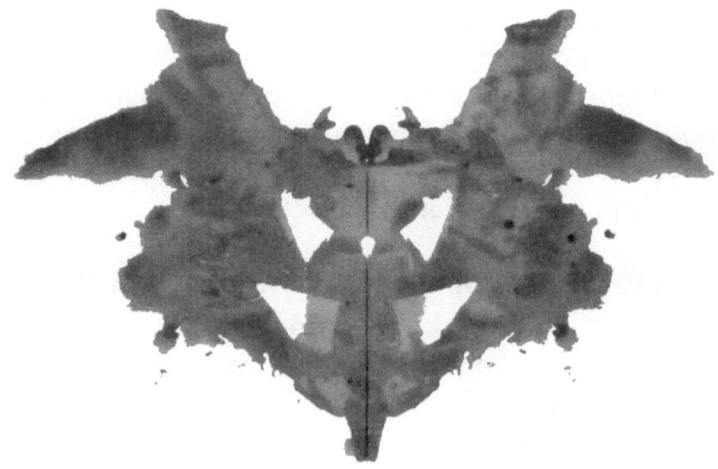

A Rorschach inkblot card

Record Setters

Misao Okawa (March 5, 1898 — April 1, 2015)

Supercentenarian Misao Okawa (大川 ミサヲ) was the world's oldest living person following the death of Jiroemon Kimura in 2013. She was the verified oldest Japanese person ever, the oldest person ever born in Asia, and the fifth oldest verified person ever recorded. She was only the fifth verified person ever to reach the age of 117, and died less than a month after her birthday. When asked for the secret of her longevity, she replied, "I wonder about that too."

Sports

Karen Muir (September 16, 1952 – April 1, 2013)

At the age of 12, South African competitive swimmer Karen Muir was the youngest person to ever break a sports record in any discipline in the 100 yard backstroke. She went on to set fifteen world records in swimming and won numerous national championships. Because of the sporting boycott of South Africa, she was unable to participate in any Olympic Games. She was elected to the International Swimming Hall of Fame in 1980.

Jack Pardee (April 19, 1936 – April 1, 2013)

Linebacker and coach Jack Pardee was the only head coach to lead teams in college football, the National Football League, the World Football League, and the Canadian Football League. He was inducted into the College Football Hall of Fame as a player in 1986.

Jo-Jo Moore (December 25, 1908 — April 1, 2001)

Left fielder Jo-Jo Moore played his entire career with the New York Giants from 1930 through 1941. Known as the "Gause Ghost" (he came from Gause, Texas), he was a career .298 hitter with 79 home runs. Although overshadowed by more colorful teammates, Moore nevertheless played in three World Series and was named to the National League All-Star Team five times.

1933 Joe "Jo-Jo" Moore baseball card

April, by Hans Thoma

April:
The Fourth Month

"I love the season well
When forest glades are teeming with bright forms,
Nor dark and many-folded clouds foretell
The coming on of storms."

— *"An April Day," Henry Wadsworth Longfellow*

The origin of the name "April" (Latin: *Aprilis*) for the fourth month of the year is uncertain. Some say that it comes from the Latin verb *aperire*, meaning "to open," a reference to springtime. A similar word in Greek, ἄνοιξις (*anoixis*, meaning "opening") also refers to spring.

On the other hand, the Romans named many months after their gods, such as "January" for Janus and "March" (*Martius*) for Mars. The month of April was sacred to the goddess Venus (Aphrodite in Greek), and thus some think that April refers to her.

The fairy tale collector Jacob Grimm suggested that April came from the Etruscan name Apru, and believed that an Etruscan god or hero of that name gave rise to the month.

The Anglo-Saxons called April *Oster-monath*, sometimes spelled *Eostur-monath*, named for the goddess Eostre. The Venerable Bede, a monk who wrote the first history of the English people, argued that Eostur was the root of the word Easter.

As the original Roman calendar started its new year in March, April was originally the second month of the year. It's uncertain when the Romans switched the new year to January, but it may have been as late as 153 BCE.

April is the springtime month in the northern
hemisphere and fall in the southern hemisphere; October
is its opposite. It's one of only four calendar months with
thirty days. Originally, April had only 29 days, but the
calendar reforms of Julius Caesar (the Julian Calendar)
added the 30th day.

The first day of April and the first day of July always
fall on the same day of the week; in leap years the first of
January also falls on the same weekday as the first of
April. In all years, the last day of April and the last day of
December fall on the same weekday.

The Jewish month of Nisan (נִיסָן) overlaps with March
and the first part of April. Months in Islam and Hindi
culture operate on a lunar cycle, and so the months slowly
migrate through the year.

April in Other Cultures

The month of April has different names in different
languages. Some nations use calendars other than the
Gregorian, and their months may overlap with April. Still,
they often have a word for April itself.

Albanian: Prill

Arabic (Egypt, Sudan, Yemen): مارأبريل (Abrīl)

Belarussian: красавік (Krasavik)

Bulgarian: април (April)

Chinese (Mandarin): 四月 (Sìyuè)

Croatian: Travanj

Czech: Duben

Finnish: Huhtikuu (burnwood month)

French: Avril

Greek: Απρίλιος (Aprílios)

Hebrew: אפריל (Âprîl)

Hindi: अप्रैल (Aprail)

Irish (Gaelic): Aibreán mí Aibreáin

Italian: Aprile

Japanese: 四月 (Shigatsu)
Korean: 사월 (Saweol)

Lithuanian: Balandis

Old English: Ēastermōnaþ

Polish: Kwiecieńc

Russian: апрель (Aprel')

Scots: Apryle

Scottish Gaelic: an Giblean

Swahili: Aprili

Thai: เมษายน (Mesayon)

Ukrainian: квітень (Kviten')

Vietnamese: Tháng tư

April Superstitions

"April showers bring May flowers."

"If early April is foggy / Rain in June will make lanes boggy."

"When April blows its horn / 'Tis good for hay and corn."

"April wet — good wheat."

"Till April's dead, change not a thread."

"Marry in May and rue the day, but marry in April if you can, joy for maiden and for man." Which day? "Monday for wealth, Tuesday for health, Wednesday the best day of all, Thursday for losses, Friday for crosses, Saturday for no luck at all."

April Symbols

Birthstone Diamond

Diamond

Birth Flowers Daisy and Sweet Pea

Daisy

Sweet Pea

April Events

Honorary Months

Presidents, Congresses, and nations around the world issue proclamations recognizing particular months to honor certain causes. These events generally fall in April. (All US unless otherwise noted.) Holidays established by states and nonprofit organizations are listed if verified.

- Alcohol Awareness Month (National Council on Alcoholism and Drug Dependence)
- Cancer Control Month
- Confederate History Month (Alabama, Florida, Georgia, Louisiana, Mississippi, Texas, Virginia)
- Earthquake Preparedness Month (California)
- Fair Housing Month
- Fresh Florida Tomato Month (Florida)
- Grange Month (National Grange)
- Holy Humor Month (Fellowship of Merry Christians)
- International Guitar Month
- Jazz Appreciation Month (Smithsonian Institution)
- Month of the Young Child® (Michigan Association for the Education of Young Children)
- National Arab-American Heritage Month
- National Autism Awareness Month (Autism Society of America)
- National Car Care Month (Car Care Council)
- National Child Abuse Prevention Month
- National Donate Life Month (Organ donations)

- National Frog Month
- National Greyhound Adoption Month
- National Kite Month (American Kiteflyers Association)
- National Landscape Architecture Month (American Society of Landscape Architects)
- National Occupational Therapy Month
- National Pecan Month (National Pecan Shellers Association)
- National Poetry Month (Academy of American Poets)
- National Poetry Writing Month (NaPoWriMo)
- National Youth Sports Safety Month (National Youth Sports Safety Foundation)
- Parkinson's Disease Awareness Month (International)
- Prevention of Animal Cruelty Month (ASPCA)
- School Library Media Month (American Library Association)
- Sexual Assault Awareness and Prevention Month (National Sexual Violence Resource Center)
- Sports Eye Safety Month (American Academy of Ophthalmology)
- Straw Hat Month

Moveable and Multi-Day Events

Some events take place over a specific week or time period. Start and finish dates may vary from year to year. Some events occur on different days each year (such as "fourth Saturday of a month").

Passover (פסח) (Judaism, Samaritanism, Saint Thomas Christians)

Passover commemorates the liberation of the Israelites from slavery in ancient Egypt around 3,300 years ago. Its story is told in the Biblical book of Exodus, which is part of both the Jewish and Samaritan Torahs and the Christian Old Testament. Exodus tells how God inflicted ten plagues upon the ancient Egyptians before the Pharaoh would release its slaves. The tenth plague killed every Egyptian first-born child. Israelites marked the doorposts of their homes with the blood of a spring lamb so that the spirit of the Lord would "pass over" the first-born in those homes. Passover is celebrated by Jews in a festive ritual dinner known as a Seder and by Samaritans with an animal sacrifice on Mount Gerizim.

For most celebrants, Passover begins on the 15th day of Nisan and ends on the 21st of Nisan in Israel and on the 22nd of Nisan outside of Israel. The earliest dates for Passover are between March 21 and March 27 (or 28), and the latest dates fall between April 20 and April 26 (or 27).

A children's Passover seder

Vesak (वैशाख) (Buddhism)

Vesak, sometimes written as Vesākha or Wesak, commemorates the birth, enlightenment, and death of Gautama Buddha, and is sometimes informally called "Buddha's Birthday." Vesak takes its name from the Asian lunisolar month of Vaisakha, and because its date comes from a different calendar, it takes place on varying dates in the Western (Gregorian) calendar, usually in April or May, although in leap years it can be celebrated in June.

On Vesak, Buddhists attend ceremonies in their local temples to sing hymns and bring offerings of flowers, candles, and joss-sticks. They typically eat only vegetarian food on that day. Birds, insects, and other animals are released in large numbers as a symbolic act of liberation. Devout Buddhists devote the day to charitable acts and to decorating their temples, and to work at following the Buddha's teachings.

In Japan, the festival is known as Hana Matsuri (花祭), and is always celebrated on April 8.

First Week of April

The first week of April can include April 1 through April 7. The first *full* week of April stretches from April 1 through April 13. The first Monday or first Friday of April can be as early as April 1 or as late as April 8. Week-long (or weekend) celebrations include:

- Alcohol Free Weekend (first weekend in April, National Council on Alcoholism and Drug Dependence)
- Golden Rule Week (International Society of Friendship and Goodwill)

A temple decorated for Vesak in Indonesia

- Laugh at Work Week
- Medication Safety Week (Women's Heart Foundation)
- National Blue Ribbon Week (National Exchange Club Foundation for the Prevention of Child Abuse)
- National Public Health Week (American Public Health Association)
- Testicular Cancer Awareness Week (National Men's Resource Center)

Opening Day (Major League Baseball)

Major League Baseball generally begins its annual season on the first Monday in April (although it has occasionally been moved to different days to keep the World Series from extending into November).

President Woodrow Wilson throws the Opening Day pitch, 1916

Easter Season

La crucifixion by El Greco

The Christian holiday of Easter in Western Christianity is held on the first Sunday after the Paschal Full Moon following the March equinox, which is officially set at March 21 by church reckoning. Easter itself can therefore occur as early as March 22 and as late as April 25, but occurs most often in April. In Eastern Christianity, which uses the Julian calendar, Easter occurs between April 4 and May 8. This also sets the date for the various events that lead up to Easter, most importantly the events of Holy Week.

Passion Sunday

The fifth Sunday of the Christian season of Lent is known as Passion Sunday in various Protestant denominations and by some traditionalist Catholics. Passion Sunday starts the two-week Passiontide, which ends on Holy Saturday, the day before Easter, commemorating the day that Jesus's body was laid in the tomb. The fifth Sunday of Lent can occur as early as March 8 (though the next time it will be that early is in 2285 CE), and as late as April 11.

Palm Sunday

The moveable feast of Palm Sunday commemorates the triumphant entry of Jesus into Jerusalem, an event mentioned in all four gospels. In many Christian churches, palm leaves are distributed to the worshippers. The earliest date for Palm Sunday is March 15, and the latest is April 18.

Maundy Thursday

The Thursday before Easter is Maundy Thursday, when the Last Supper took place. Because of its relation to Easter, the earliest day it can occur is March 19, and the latest it can occur is April 22.

Good Friday

Good Friday, observed during Holy Week on the Friday preceding Easter Sunday, commemorates the crucifixion of Jesus and his death at Calvary. Because of its relation to Easter, the earliest day it can occur is March 20, and the latest it can occur is April 23.

Holy Saturday

Sometimes called Easter Eve or Black Saturday, Holy Saturday commemorates the day in which Jesus's body lay in the tomb. Some mistakenly refer to this day as "Easter Saturday," but that properly describes the Saturday following Easter, the last day of Easter Week. The earliest it can occur is March 21, and the latest it can occur is April 24.

Easter

Easter celebrates the resurrection of Jesus Christ on the third day after his crucifixion. In the liturgical calendar, Easter follows the season of Lent, and begins the period known as Eastertide, which ends on Pentecost Sunday.

Easter is observed religiously in a morning service. In the U.S., it's also common to decorate

Easter eggs and make Easter baskets of eggs and candy, often with the Easter bunny as a symbol. The White House traditionally hosts an egg hunt, and many communities have Easter parades.

Easter customs around the world include bonfires (Cyprus, western Sweden), men spanking women with a ceremonial whip (Czech Republic and Slovakia), egg fighting (Bulgaria), cross-country skiing and reading murder mysteries (Norway), and children dressed as witches collecting candy door-to-door (other Nordic countries).

Easter Eggs

Easter Monday

In some Roman Catholic and Eastern Orthodox cultures, the Monday after Easter is celebrated as a holiday. It is also known as Egg Nyte, featuring egg rolling competitions and dousing other people with water that had been blessed with holy water the previous day at mass. Easter Monday is also celebrated as Family Day in South Africa. In Guyana, people fly kites that were made on Holy Saturday. In Portugal, it is known as the Anjo (Ivy) Festival, in which people picnic in the countryside.

Śmigus-Dyngus (Poland, Hungary, Czech Republic, Slovakia)

The Monday after Easter in Poland and in the Polish diaspora is known as Śmigus-Dyngus, or simply Dyngus Day in the US. Boys throw water over girls they like and spank them with pussy willows. Girls avoid getting wet by giving boys "ransoms" of painted eggs.

Easter Week (Western Christianity), Bright Week (Eastern Christianity)

The period from Easter Sunday to the following Saturday is known as Easter Week. In both Western and Eastern Christianity (where it's known as Bright Week), the resurrection continues to be celebrated in church services. Easter Tuesday is a public holiday in the Australian state of Tasmania.

Egg Salad Week (American Egg Board)

Egg Salad Week celebrates the many ways to use all the Easter eggs gathered on the holiday, normally celebrated the week following Easter Sunday.

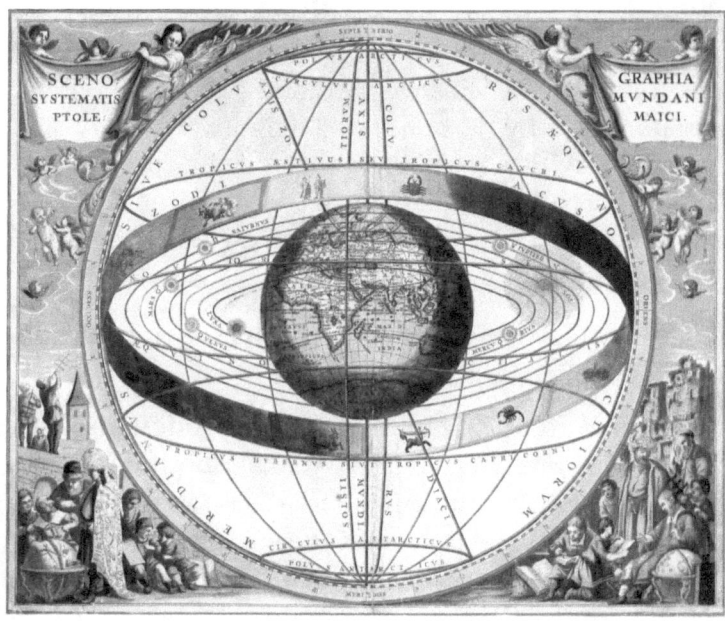

Scenography of the Ptolemaic Cosmography, by Johannes van Loon, based on Andreas Cellarius's *Harmonia Macrocosmica,* 1660

April Zodiac Signs

From the perspective of someone on Earth, the Sun appears to move through the sky throughout the year, along a path astronomers call the *ecliptic plane*. The ecliptic plane is divided into twelve constellations, known as the zodiac, based on traditionally observed patterns of stars. On your birthday, you can't see your constellation, because it's in the daytime sky.

The zodiac was first developed by Babylonian astronomers about 2,500 years ago. Because they were unaware that the Earth wobbles like a spinning top (known as *precession*), they didn't make allowance for the fact that the Sun's path through the zodiac changes over time.

That means there are now two sets of dates for your birth sign. The *tropical dates* are the original Babylonian dates; the *sidereal dates* tell you where the Sun actually appears as it moves along its annual path.

For April 1, the sidereal sign is **Pisces**, and the tropical sign is **Aries.**

Pisces

Tropical February 20 to March 20
Sidereal March 15 to April 14

In the Roman legend of Venus and her son Cupid, they escaped the clutches of Typhon, known as the "father of all monsters," by transforming into fish and tying themselves together with rope. That's why the name Pisces is plural for fish. The constellation appears as a somewhat ragged "V" shape, representing the rope, with the "fish" located at the two rope ends.

In astrology, Pisces is a water sign, compatible with the other water signs Cancer and Scorpio, as well as with the earth signs Taurus, Virgo, and Capricorn. Pisceans are supposed to be imaginative, compassionate, unworldly, secretive, and escapist.

Aries

Tropical March 21 to April 19
Sidereal April 15 to May 15

In Greek mythology, Aries is a ram with golden wings and golden wool who rescued the twins Phrixus and Helle from certain death. Although Helle died in the rescue attempt, the grateful Phrixus sacrificed the ram to Zeus. The golden fleece from the sacrificed ram played a prominent part in the later myth of Jason and the Argonauts.

In astrology, Aries, a fire sign, is compatible with the other fire signs of Gemini, Leo, and Sagittarius, and to a lesser extent with air signs Scorpio and Libra. Arians are supposed to be adventurous, enthusiastic, quick-tempered, and impulsive.

Illustration by Edward Penfield

What Day of the Week is April 1?

On what day of the week does April 1 fall?

Surprisingly, this isn't an easy question. Because the calendar year is 365 days long (366 in leap years), it doesn't divide evenly by the seven days of the week.

Also, the Earth goes around the Sun in about 365-1/4 days, so a calendar tends to drift over time. That's why the same date falls on different weekdays in different years.

This is made even more complicated by a change in calendars that took place in 1582. Our modern calendar has its roots in ancient Rome, in a calendar reform conducted by Julius Caesar. Caesar commissioned mathematicians to attack the problem, and they came up with the idea of leap years, and thus standardized the calendar for centuries to come. This was called the Julian calendar.

Over time, however, the small errors in Caesar's calculation compounded. That's why Pope Gregory XIII commissioned the Gregorian calendar, used in most of the world today. Some countries converted in 1582, when the calendar was first developed; some converted later; other still haven't changed.

Gregorian and Julian aren't the only types of calendars. The Hebrew year, the Islamic year, and many other calendars are used in different parts of the world and among different people.

You can convert Gregorian dates to other calendars, including the Hebrew calendar, the Islamic calendar, and even the Mayan calendar by visiting the Fourmilab Calendar Converter at http://www.fourmilab.ch/documents/calendar/.

Chinese calendar systems are quite complex and have changed several times; a full discussion is far beyond the scope of this book. If you're interested, you can find information here: http://www.hermetic.ch/cal_stud/chinese_cal.htm.

On Names and Dates

Historians use "CE" (Common Era) and "BCE" (Before the Common Era) instead of the more common "AD" (Anno Domini, or Year of Our Lord) and "BC" (Before Christ), reflecting the fact that the year-numbering system established by the Gregorian calendar is used throughout the world in many countries not culturally Christian.

The CE/BCE designation dates back to at least 1708, and has been adopted as a standard by the United Nations and the Universal Postal Union. Because this series of books covers events and people of all nations and cultures, we use the CE/BCE terms.

The abbreviation "O.S." ("Old Style") on some dates refers to the fact that the Russian Empire did not switch from the Julian to the Gregorian calendar at the same time as the rest of Europe, and therefore some figures and events have two dates.

Also, in the Julian calendar in England in the 16th century, the year began on March 25 rather than January 1. To avoid confusion with Gregorian dates, dates between January and March were often written using both years.

People and events whose original names are not in the Western alphabet have their native names (where possible) in the appropriate script shown in parenthesis. If you are using an e-reader to access an electronic version of this book, all characters don't always display on all devices.

A 50-year brass perpetual calendar.

Cartoon by John T. McCutcheon

Copyright, Credit, and Contact

Follow Us

For a complete list of titles, visit our website at timespinnerpress.com. Our blog Dobson's Improbable History (http://improbhistory.blogspot.com) features short articles on events and people associated with each day, and updates several times each week. You can also get a daily "What Happened In History" message and all the latest Timespinner Press news by following us on Facebook at https://www.facebook.com/TimespinnerPress. Our Twitter feed @SidewiseThinker links you to all our News of the Day.

Contact Us

Find an error or a format problem? Want information about the series, about us, or about when the volume for your special day might be available? Please email us at editor@timespinnerpress.com. (We also take requests if your special day isn't yet complete. Please give us at least six weeks' notice if possible.)

Sources

We owe a great debt to Wikipedia, which is our first stop for research. We attempt to make independent confirmation of all important dates and facts through a variety of other sources. Other sources we frequently use include the Library of Congress; "on this day" listings from *Encyclopedia Britannica*, the *New York Times*, and the BBC; Omniglot for the names of months in other languages; *Chase's Calendar of Events* and the website Brownielocks; and, of course, the always essential Google.

All art and photographs are either in the public domain, used under a Creative Commons license, or with a "fair use" justification, and most frequently come from Wikimedia Commons and the Library of Congress Prints and Photographs Division.

Attribution is provided where possible, or as requested by the copyright owner, or when there is particular historical significance, listed below. For information about any particular illustration or photograph, please contact us.

Credits

- The cover image is a French April Fool's postcard from the early years of the 20th century. It is in the public domain because its copyright has expired.

- The illustration of the month of April used on the back cover and as the frontispiece is from the French Gothic illuminated manuscript *Les Très Riches Heures du duc de Berry* by the Limbourg Brothers, Jean Colombe, and an intermediate painter whose name is lost to history. It is in the public domain because its copyright has expired. It has been cropped and its color and contrast have been adjusted for use in this book.

- The 1894 painting of Otto von Bismarck is by Franz von Lenbach, and is in the public domain because its copyright has expired.

- The photograph of a subway car appearing to break through the pavement was taken by Lars Andersen, who released the image into the public domain. Note the sign "Gevalia" and the accident site tape with the words "Uventede gæster?" ("Unexpected guests?"). Gevalia coffee's advertising featured various vehicles popping up with unexpected guests.

- The fake admission ticket to the "Washing the Lions" ceremony at the Tower of London is in the public domain because its copyright has expired.

- The "edible book" version of Ray Bradbury's *Fahrenheit 451* was displayed at the 2012 International Edible Book Festival. The photograph was taken by Hal B. Klein for 90.5 WESA, and is used here under CC BY-SA 2.0.

- The 2009 photograph of the US Air Force Academy cadet chapel was taken by A. Hodges, who released the work into the public domain.

- The wood engraving titled "The Steam-ship 'Atlantic,' Wrecked on Mars Head on the Morning of April 1, 1873," was published in the April 1873 issue of *Harper's Weekly*. It is in the public domain because its copyright has expired.

- The photograph of American LCTs unloading supplies on Yellow Beach in April 1945 is in the public domain as a work created by an officer or employee of the US Federal government as part of that person's official duties.

- The photograph of U.S. Navy Douglas R4D and U.S. Air Force C-47 aircraft unload at Tempelhof Airport during the Berlin Airlift is in the public domain as a work created by an officer or employee of the US Federal government as part of that person's official duties.

- The photograph of Earth from outer space, taken by the satellite TIROS-1 is in the public domain as a work solely created by NASA.

- The photograph of Comet Hale-Bopp is in the public domain as a work solely created by NASA.

- The publicity still of Debbie Reynolds was taken sometime before 1964. Publicity photos have traditionally not been copyrighted. Since they are disseminated to the public, they are generally considered public domain, and therefore clearance by the studio that produced them is not necessary.

- The movie poster for the 1950 Japanese film *Shubun (Scandal)* is in the public domain under Japanese copyright law, but retains its US copyright. It is used here under "fair use" standards to illustrate a biographical sketch of a significant person, no free equivalent is easily available, and the reproduction quality is too low to create counterfeit goods.

- The scan still of Lon Chaney in the 1925 film *Phantom of the Opera* is in the public domain because it was published in the United States between 1923 and 1963 and although there may or may not have been a copyright notice, the copyright was not renewed.

- The photograph of Sergei Rachmaninoff is a press photograph from the George Grantham Bain collection, which was purchased by the Library of Congress in 1948. According to the library, there are no known restrictions on the use of these photos. The date of the photograph is unknown, probably sometime in the 1910s or 1920s.

- The creator of the graphic of Maslow's Hierarchy of Needs, Tom W. Sulcer, has released the work into the public domain.

- The 1973 photograph of Marvin Gaye is from a trade advertisement for his album *Anthology,* first published in *Billboard*. It is in the public domain because it was first published in the United States between 1923 and 1977 without a copyright notice. The photographer is unknown.

- The 1922 portrait of Martha Graham is by Nickolas Muray. It is in the public domain because its first publication occurred prior to January 1, 1923, and its copyright has expired.

- The 1937 publicity photograph from the series *Fibber McGee and Molly* was published in a two-page ad for NBC Radio that appeared in *Life* Magazine, April 12, 1937. It is in the public domain because it was first published in the United States between 1923 and 1977 without a copyright notice. The photographer is unknown.

- The Rorschach inkblot card is in the public domain because its copyright has expired.

- The painting "April" is from the calendar book *Festkalender* by Hans Thoma. It is in the public domain because its copyright has expired.

- The photograph of two diamonds grown by Washington Diamonds was taken by Inbai-Tania Studio, and is used here under the CC BY-SA 3.0 license.

- The photograph of a daisy (*Bellis perennis*) was taken by André Karwath and is used here under the CC BY-SA 2.5 license.

- The photograph of President Woodrow Wilson throwing the ball on the opening day of baseball season 1916 is a press photograph from the National Photo Company Collection, part of the Library of Congress Prints and Photographs Division, and is in the public domain because it was published prior to January 1, 1923.

- The painting *La crucifixión* by El Greco is located in the Museo del Prado. It is in the public domain because its copyright has expired.

- The photograph of Czechoslovakian Easter eggs was taken by Jan Kameníček, who has released the image into the public domain.

- The illustration "Scenography of the Ptolemaic Cosmography," by Johannes van Loon, is based on Andreas Cellarius's *Harmonia Macrocosmica*, published in 1660. It is in the public domain because its copyright has expired.

- The photograph of the 1906 automobile calendar by Edward Penfield is from the Library of Congress Prints and Photographs Division, and is in the public domain because it was published prior to January 1, 1923.

- The 50-year perpetual calendar photograph is in the public domain.

- The cartoon by John T. McCutcheon is from his 1905 collection *The Mysterious Stranger and Other Cartoons* by John T. McCutcheon. It is in the public domain because its copyright has expired.

License Description and Terms

Aside from material purely in the public domain, photographs and other material in this book are used under specific licenses permitting free use, usually with an attribution requirement. For full text and terms of these licenses, click or enter the appropriate links below. If you believe there is an error in the copyright status or attribution of any of these images, please email us.

Timespinner
Press